Connect,
Compute,
and
Compete

The Report of the California
Education Technology
Task Force

Publishing Information

Connect, Compute, and Compete: The Report of the California Education Technology Task Force was published by the California Department of Education, 721 Capitol Mall, Sacramento, California (mailing address: P.O. Box 944272, Sacramento, CA 94244-2720). It was distributed under the provisions of the Library Distribution Act and *Government Code* Section 11096.

ISBN 0-8011-1281-8

Ordering Information

Copies of this publication are available for $5.75 each, plus shipping and handling charges. California residents are charged sales tax. Orders may be sent to the Bureau of Publications, Sales Unit, California Department of Education, P.O. Box 271, Sacramento, CA 95812-0271; FAX (916) 323-0823. See page 30 for more complete information on ordering.

A partial list of educational resources available form the Department appears on pages 29–30. In addition, an illustrated *Educational Resources Catalog* describing publications, videos, and other instructional media available from the Department can be obtained without charge by writing to the address given above or by calling the Sales Unit at (916) 445-1260.

Contents

Acknowledgments

California Education Technology Task Force Members

Bernie Hargadon, Co-Chair; former President, McKesson International
Barbara O'Connor, Co-Chair; Director, Institute for the Study
of Politics and Media, California State University, Sacramento

Greg Ballard, President, CAPCOM Entertainment
David Brown, Superintendent, Napa Valley Unified School District
George Buchanan, Director, Business Communications, Hughes
Electronics Corporation
David Byer, Education Policy Manager, Software Publishers Association
Martha Connellan, Vice President, School Products, Davidson and
Associates, Inc.
Terry Crane, Senior Vice President, WW Strategic Market Segments,
Apple Computer, Inc.
Peter Cross, Senior Vice President of Engineering, Bay Networks, Inc.
Jan Davidson, President, Davidson and Associates, Inc.
John Detwiler, President, The Detwiler Foundation
John Gage, Director, Science Office, Sun Micro Systems
Ron Garcia, Administrator/Associate Director, Migrant Education,
Region 8
*Charles Garvin**, Chairman, Telescan Systems, Inc.
Pat Hanlon, English Teacher, Lowell High School, San Francisco Unified
School District; Member, Technology Committee, California Federa-
tion of Teachers
Jim Henderson, Program Manager, Academic and Community
Relations, IBM
Roger Hoyer, Assistant Superintendent for Technology, New Haven
Unified School District
Jerry Hume, Board Member, California State Board of Education
John Kernan, Chairman and Chief Executive Officer, The Lightspan
Partnership, Inc.
Pamela Korporaal, President, Computer Using Educators, Inc.; and
Technology Specialist, Norwalk-La Mirada Unified School District
Wendy Lazarus, Director, The Children's Partnership

*Subgroup chair.

Robert Lee, President of Business Communication Services, Pacific Bell

Elia Leon, Marketing Program Integrator, Hewlett-Packard

Marc B. Liebman, Superintendent, Laguna Salada Union Elementary
School District

John Lindsay, Assistant Superintendent, Educational Services,
Kern County Office of Education

Melinda Luedtke, Vice President, J. P. Morgan Securities, Inc.

Bill MacAllister, Technical Marketing Manager, Innosoft
International, Inc.

Dennis Mangers, Senior Vice President, California Cable Television
Association

Steve Mayer, Community Member

David P. Meaney, Superintendent, Sacramento County Office
of Education

Kathleen Milnes, Vice President, Public Affairs Coalition
of the Alliance of Motion Picture and Television Producers

Ted Mitchell, Dean, UCLA Graduate School of Education

Homer S. Montalvo, Associate Dean, California State University,
Bakersfield

David Moore, Executive Vice-President, Kelmoore Investment Company,
Inc.

*__Ellen Nelson__, Chairman of the Board, Decision Development Corporation

Flynn Nogueira, Director, Market Response, GTE

Chet Pipkin, President, Belkin Components

Bill Ragsdale, Mentor Teacher, California Teachers Association

Cathy Simon, Principal, Simon, Martin-Vegue, Winklestein, and Morris

Pete Sinclair, President and Chief Executive Officer, Smart Valley, Inc.

*__Lewis Solmon__, President, Milken Institute for Job & Capital Formation

*__Lawrence J. Stupski__, Vice Chairman, The Charles Schwab Corporation

Bill Tauscher, Chairman and Chief Executive Officer, Vanstar
Corporation

Glenn Umetsu, Vice President, Network Operations, AT&T Wireless
Services

Don Vial, Senior Advisor, California Foundation for Environment
and Economy

AJ Willmer, Member, Board of Education, Beverly Hills Unified School
District

Department of Education Staff

Janice Lowen Agee, Writer, Executive Services

Ann M. Evans, Director, School Facilities Planning Division

Chris Hartnett, Analyst, Education Technology Office

Donavan Merck, Manager, Education Technology Office

William Padia, Assistant Superintendent, Research, Evaluation,
and Technology Division

Carole Teach, Manager, K–12 Network Planning

Cheryl Tiner, Analyst, Research, Evaluation, and Technology Division

---

*Subgroup chairs.

Jan Volkoff, Consultant, Research, Evaluation, and Technology Division
Frank Wallace, Consultant, Education Technology Office
Richard Whitmore, Deputy Superintendent, Finance, Technology,
and Planning Branch

Special Thanks

Kalyani Chirra, Research Assistant, Milken Institute for Job & Capital
Formation
Rick Normington, Area Vice President, Pacific Bell
Steve Palmer, Education Market Development Executive,
Apple Computer, Inc.

For report production:
Apple Computer, Inc.
AT&T
California Cable Television Association
GTE
IBM
Pacific Bell

Consultants

Nikki Green, Green & Green
Monique Jordan, President, Applied Concepts
Brenda Kempster, President, Kempster Group

Additional Participants

Tony Armstrong, Director, Governmental Affairs, GTE
Bill Bondy, Associate Architect, Simon, Martin-Vegue, Winklestein,
and Morris
John Cradler, Program Director, Educational Technology, WestEd
Cheryl Fagnano, Vice President of Educational Research, Milken
Institute for Job & Capital Formation
John Thomas Flynn, Chief Information Officer, Department of
Information Technology
Eric Garen, President, Learning Tree International
Dave Lenehan, Government Affairs, AT&T
Dean Nafziger, Executive Director, WestEd
Robert Nolan, Director, Alternative Education, Napa Valley Unified
School District
Ray Reinhard, Deputy Secretary, Governor's Office of Child
Development and Education
Kevin Rocap, Co-Director, Pacific Southwest Regional Technology
Consortium
Leslie Saul, Director, Smart Valley, Inc.
Daniel Weiler, Vice President, RPP International, Inc.
Lynn Wright, Deputy Chief, Department of Information Technology

Introduction

ANY nine year old who has ever commandeered her parents' computer to surf the Internet, asked a NASA scientist about acid rain, or designed a multimedia language arts project knows what dozens of blue-ribbon panels have concluded in vastly more syllables: "Computers are cool!"

Technology has the power to teach, to motivate, to captivate, and to transform an ordinary classroom into a training ground for the next generation of artists, entrepreneurs, and government leaders. Unfortunately, California's schoolchildren have far less technology than they need to take their rightful place in tomorrow's information society. An estimated 60 percent of all jobs in the United States by the year 2000 will require a working knowledge of information technologies.

Even today, where would many workers be without a computer and the links it provides to information? Now, imagine how we are handicapping public school children by sending them to "work" each day without the tools many of us take for granted.

Surveys of California businesses indicate that the majority of 1997 high school seniors will graduate unprepared for the rigors of the workplace. Moreover, 12 years from now, when today's first graders move into the job market or on to college, technology will be even more pervasive and sophisticated than it is today. What will the gap in job preparedness be then?

Our purpose in this report is not to build a case regarding the virtues of computers in the classroom. We're convinced. What we have

1

taken on is the business of integrating technology into California classrooms by setting what we consider to be realistic goals for the process, assessing the cost, and proposing a pragmatic strategy for getting there.

We don't presume that technology is the only issue worthy of attention when it comes to public instruction. Many factors influence education policies, among them class size, teachers' salaries, hours of classroom instruction, and adequate facilities. A discussion of those factors, however, is beyond the scope of this report.

Instead, our research has led us to the conclusion that, more than any other single measure, computers and network technologies, properly implemented, will bolster California's continuing efforts to right what's wrong with our public schools. While schools have made progress, much more still needs to be done.

This is a blueprint for action.

The Task Force

In October, 1995, Delaine Eastin, State Superintendent of Public Instruction, convened our task force to study the challenge of integrating technology into California's kindergarten through twelfth-grade classrooms. Our team consisted of 46 members, including business executives, educators, and representatives of organizations, foundations, and communities.

We were charged with answering the following questions:

- What is the current state of technological readiness in California's classrooms and school libraries?
- What infrastructure, equipment, and support do we need?
- How much will it cost?
- Where should the money come from?

Where Are We Now?

California's disinvestment in classroom and library computers and telecommunications infrastructure has left our state lagging other states by most measures of technology. A 1995 report of a survey conducted by Quality Education Data, Inc., comparing

California with other states found the Golden State tarnished in its rankings:

✓ 36th in CD-ROMs
✓ 43rd in network access
✓ 45th in number of students per computer
✓ 50th in videocassette recorders

Even an item as commonplace in most homes as the telephone is virtually nonexistent in California's classrooms. So it is not surprising that nearly 14 students vie for each computer in California classrooms, compared with about six students in the states which boast the country's best student-to-computer ratios. Worse yet, closer examination of the statistics reveals that many of the computers counted in the survey were outmoded models incapable of running current software or linking to a wide-area network.

Discounting obsolete equipment, California should more accurately count one computer for every 73 students.

Technology is not the only place where our schools fall behind. For example, the National Assessment of Educational Progress ranked the state's elementary school children last among children in 39 states reporting fourth-grade reading performance.

Admittedly, the case for asserting a cause-and-effect relationship between integrated classroom technology and improved student performance is sometimes anecdotal. Politics and practicality make it impossible to randomly assign technology to one group of students while denying it to another. Thus, the study of classroom technology probably will never lend itself to the rigors of the scientific investigation once accorded the polio vaccine, for example.

Even states with advanced technology and diligent record keeping have had neither in place for enough time to bear long-term results. Nor have any states instituted programs as comprehensive or as broad based as those we propose.

Yet there is much evidence regarding technology's value for students in acquiring the skills demanded by employers as well as in improving student achievement. For that reason it is important to look at some things we *do* know and to become advocates for technology:

• A 1995 survey of more than 100 recent academic studies indicated that technology-based instruction had significantly improved student performance in English–language arts, math, history–social science, and science.

The information and technology explosion will offer . . . to the young people of the future more opportunities and challenges than any generation of Americans has ever seen.

President Bill Clinton

Kids may be young, but they're not saps. They've been to the mall where every clerk has a computer and a phone. We tell our children school is important, but too often the school doesn't look important.

Delaine Eastin, State Superintendent of Public Instruction

- The U.S. military found that trainees had reached required competencies in 30 percent less time with computer-based instruction than with standard methods.
- A computer pilot program targeted to remedial students in New York City demonstrated 80 percent gains in reading and 90 percent in math.

If we were to hypothesize the kind of school best able to enhance students' learning by incorporating technology, we would likely call to mind Clear View Elementary School or classrooms in the Hueneme Elementary School District.

Clear View Elementary School
Chula Vista, California

A LOOK AHEAD Eight miles from the Mexican border, 575 children attend Clear View Elementary School. Most come from low-income families, including many newly arrived immigrants. English is a new language for 68 percent of the youngsters.

Since 1991 Principal Ginger Hovenic has worked to secure educational grant money and donations from the business community to purchase computers; equip the school with fiber, satellite, and cable communications; and invest in training for teachers and administrators. As part of a joint venture with San Diego State University, Clear View is designated a professional development school where student teachers receive experience in an innovative classroom.

In a science lesson, for example, a group of Clear View students collaborated with students from around the country to collect data on local weather conditions while others worked with an electron microscope 26 miles away under the direction of a professor at San Diego State University. Clear View history students wrote and published a book on Supreme Court Justice John Marshall.

Another class collaborated with students in Rhode Island, Nebraska, and England to study V-E Day. Even first graders know how to use computers to "drive" a scale model car they built from LEGOs™ through their model LEGO™ town. And administrators use E-mail, accessible 24 hours a day, to communicate with parents, teachers, and students about homework assignments, school events, and other news.

Hueneme Elementary School District
Port Hueneme, California

A VIEW OF A MODEL PROGRAM Sixty-five miles north of Los Angeles, the Hueneme Elementary School District has produced profound changes in student learning environments through the use of interactive, networked technology. Port Hueneme is a community of

W e see computers as . . . tools to promote thinking on the part of students and teachers. . . . [Children who graduate from our elementary school] are pushing the bar at middle school.

Ginger Hovenic, Principal
Clear View Elementary School

4

racial, linguistic, and economic diversity. Over the past decade the school district has used state grant seed money, local resources, and help from private industry to fuel an aggressive research and development program combining technology with a focus on student learning. The district has created networked "smart classrooms," which provide a seamless integration of dissimilar data, audio, and video learning resources to teachers and students.

All 11 schools, plus the district office and maintenance facilities, have local area networks that are linked to the World Wide Web. Each classroom has a telephone, and each teacher has voice mail, which can be used for parent communication.

Both junior high schools have direct connections to Lawrence Livermore Laboratory's computers, which allow students to review alternative strategies for solving complex math and science projects.

Another network donated and maintained by the local cable company provides for a multiple integration of audio and video among all district classrooms. Each school also participates with a national school partner connected by United States Department of Defense communication lines.

More recently, Hueneme has explored the potential of distance learning and telecommunications and has established classroom-to-classroom and school-to-school networks within Hueneme and across the nation. Currently, Hueneme teachers are working directly with private industry researchers, using state-of-the-art technology to author a CD-ROM interactive electronic curriculum that brings the sophistication of multimedia networks to any school or learner with access to a CD-ROM player and the Internet. Potential revenues from this joint venture will provide direct compensation for the teachers involved and a continuing stream of revenue to fund future district research and development projects.

However, of greatest importance, the approximately 8,000 Hueneme learners have responded dramatically to technology. According to Superintendent Ronald Rescigno, students are achieving far beyond their peers in similar communities in California.

To use technology to promote school reform is like flying with a tailwind.

Howard Mehlinger, Director
Center for Excellence in Education
Indiana University

Timeline

THE CLOCK IS TICKING Every year in which we fail to improve student access to computers and telecommunications equipment, our children fall farther and farther behind. Even if it were magically possible to blanket our schools and homes with technology in one stroke, teachers would remain insufficiently trained to make optimal use of the equipment. And schools would still lack the courseware needed to adapt the new learning tools to core curricula. *That's why we propose a program timeline of four years.*

California competes with other states—and nations—for an economic edge by preparing its schools and students for the rigors of the Information Age. A four-year horizon allows us to start at once raising the funds required to ramp up hardware and software acquisition, classroom connectivity, and the necessary staff development beginning in 1997. Simultaneously, we anticipate that private industry will accelerate the development of software based on the state's curriculum frameworks, which guide instruction, as the market for these products grows.

The recommendations that follow are designed to stage in basic equipment and the capacity to use it by the year 2000, at which time we expect to have achieved four all-important objectives:

- A student-to-computer ratio of four to one (see Figure 1)
- Telecommunications access for students in every classroom and library (see Figure 2)
- Technology as an integral resource for all students and teachers
- Reading and math scores above the 50th percentile nationally

How do we get there from here?

FIGURE 1

Benefit: Fewer Students per Computer

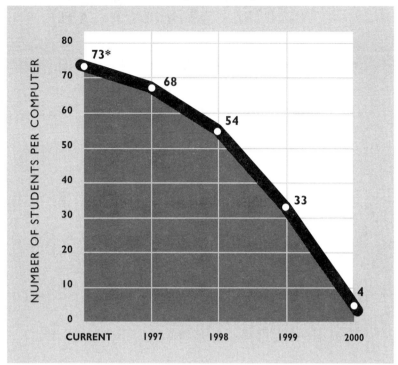

*Outmoded computers incapable of running current software or linking to networks are not included.

FIGURE 2

Benefit: More Students with Internet Access

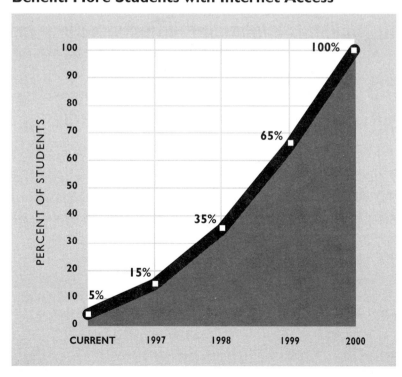

Recommendations

Telecommunications Infrastructure, Hardware, and Learning Resources

I Equip every California classroom and school library with the technology resources needed to create a learning environment that will improve student achievement.

In an arena changing as rapidly as technology, a too-rigid definition of equipment or material standards risks "fighting the last war." To avoid creating a Maginot Line through our classrooms, we choose to focus on functionality rather than on specific device features or attributes which would quickly become obsolete. The recommendations that follow represent benchmarks for technological resources rather than a final destination. Although other states will also undoubtedly increase their efforts to integrate technology into their classrooms, we believe that attaining these benchmarks will bring us into the top 10 percent of states. From here we hope classrooms will adjust their technology upward in support of specific curricula and classroom needs.

The acquisition of the recommended telecommunications infrastructure, hardware, and learning resources will make possible viewing video presentations in individual, classroom, and small-group settings; running animation-based simulations; accessing the Internet with evolving digital capability; and preparing multimedia presentations with full-motion and still-frame animation linked to the curriculum. It will also facilitate communication between and among school constituencies: parents, teachers, students, and administrators.

Specifically, we recommend the following:

Telecommunications Infrastructure

- Equip every classroom and school library with the telecommunications capability to support interactive, high-speed transmission of full-motion video, voice, and data.

Hardware

- In every classroom provide:
  - Six to eight networked multimedia computers with high-quality monitors and headphones
  - Special interfaces for persons with disabilities
  - Scanner
  - Networked laser printer
  - 27-inch or larger television monitor
  - Overhead projector and screen
  - Telephone
  - Furniture and security equipment

- For every five classrooms provide:
  - Color printer
  - Audio recorder and player
  - Liquid crystal presentation panel
  - Videocassette recorder and player
  - Videodisc player
  - Video capture board
  - Video camera

- For every 15 classrooms provide:
  - Fax machine
  - High-speed copier

Learning Resources

Although we do not recommend particular technology-based learning resources in this report, we do recommend the revamping

As increasingly capable machines join Americans at the workplace —join them as both coworkers and competitors—the payoff to education and training has soared, and the penalty for lacking skills has stiffened.

Robert Reich, United States Secretary of Labor

One in four California teachers reports using textbooks that are more than ten years old.

Survey of the Association of American Publishers and the National Education Association

of the current instructional resources adoption process. The process by which the California State Board of Education currently adopts instructional materials is insufficient to the task of evaluating and acquiring technology-based learning resources. Formulated for an earlier era that was dominated by printed texts, the adoption process is unable to accommodate either the short-term publication cycle or the highly focused nature of courseware, CD-ROM, or video resources.

Specifically, we recommend the following:

- Adopt a shorter submission cycle.
- Include supplementary materials, not only full courses of study.
- Improve reviewers' technology expertise.
- Establish a network of Web sites for statewide exchange of information regarding learning resources and their effective use in classrooms.
- Set standards for site licensing of software.
- Implement an on-line "consumer report" for educational resources accessible by students and parents.

Student Content and Performance Standards

2 Incorporate technology into student content and performance standards recommended by the state for adoption at the district level.

In October, 1995, Assembly Bill 265 created a Commission for the Establishment of Academic Content and Performance Standards, charged with developing standards that could be required before a high school diploma is awarded.

Specifically, we recommend the following:

- Extend the mission of this oversight body to include technology-based proficiencies embedded in each content area, at each grade level, and in the design of acceptable mechanisms for testing levels of technology performance, including:
  - Facility with computers and software, such as word processing programs
  - Ability to use technology to organize and prioritize complex problem-solving tasks
  - Ability to access and gather information from electronic data sources

- Use indicators in addition to test scores to measure the overall improvement expected to result from widespread technology integration. For example, businesses can be surveyed to determine their satisfaction with students' job preparedness. Other indicators that must be made part of an annual census are dropout rates, parent participation, attendance, advanced-course enrollment, and participation in scholastic extra-curricular activities.

- Require the California Department of Education, as part of a continuous school improvement program, to collect and publish an annual report of technology-related performance statistics not only to benchmark results but also to target additional resources where needed. Such information should be made available at local, state, and national levels.

Technology is a very important part of today's [education] basics.

Richard Riley, United States
Secretary of Education

Students learn nothing when they recopy, but they learn a great deal when they revise; that is, when they take time to see their work in a new way. . . . With the added components of graphics, desktop publishing, and other creative uses of technology, writing becomes truly rewarding.

Kaki Logan, Teacher
Pat Gemma, Principal
Alhambra High School
Martinez, California

Teacher Content and Performance Standards

3 Integrate technology into the content and performance standards that will be used as the basis for setting policies for preparing, hiring, evaluating, and promoting teachers.

The ability of teachers to use technology to promote students' acquisition of basic skills and subject-matter content is critical to education's success. Accomplishing this objective requires front-end preparation as well as ongoing training opportunities and incentives.

Specifically, we recommend the following:

- Establish a three-tier scale for evaluating technology competency and use it to monitor attainment of site-specific goals

  Level One—Personal Proficiency: ability to use technology for personal use

  Level Two—Instructional Proficiency: ability to incorporate technology into teaching and learning

  Level Three—Leadership Proficiency: ability to train colleagues to reach Level One and Level Two proficiencies

- Make grants available for staff development within district guidelines.

- Negotiate additional stipends or salary schedule increments for teachers who acquire Level Two and Level Three skills.

- Encourage teacher education programs to train prospective teachers in the use of technology and its integration into their subject areas.

- Encourage students and teachers to act as mentors to enhance technology skills.

- Explore the possibility of requiring Level Two proficiency for new teachers and requiring current teachers to attain Level One proficiency within two years and Level Two proficiency within five years.

A congressionally mandated review of 47 comparisons of multimedia instruction with more conventional approaches to instruction found time savings of 30 percent, improved achievement, and cost savings of 30 to 40 percent . . . .

United States Advisory Council on the National Information Infrastructure

Technical Support

4 **Provide the expertise and resources needed to support the effective use of technology by students, teachers, parents, and the broader community.**

Anyone who has ever used a computer knows that sometimes things go wrong. When problems do occur, most users have no access to assistance unless they have an expert friend or the number of an industry help line.

Schools with newer hardware may find adequate technical support with one technician per 300 computers. Those schools using older installations or those with more challenging needs may require support closer to general industry guidelines, which call for one technician for every 50 workstations.

Specifically, we recommend the following:

- Provide a referral service that includes dial-up help lines, technology specialists, mentors, published materials, and on-site visits to assist in solving technical problems.
- Extend technical assistance to parents and the greater school community by establishing and staffing community technical assistance centers.
- Make facilities and technical support available to parents and the community during evening hours and on weekends.
- Establish on-line services for frequently asked questions regarding widespread applications.
- Encourage development of newsgroups and chat rooms for discussing specific curriculum and problem issues.

California's schools . . . need to adopt some of the ways [leading edge] companies do business. Like companies that are thriving in the face of pressure on costs and performance, government should look beyond increasing efficiency of existing functions and work toward cost-effective results.

The Governor's Council on Information Technology

Costs

There is no argument that putting technology into more than 200,000 California classrooms and school libraries is a massive undertaking. Although some benefits in improved productivity will be realized almost immediately, most children coming into the system today will not enter the labor force for at least 15 years. Bringing California classrooms from the back of the pack to a position of leadership among states integrating technology into classroom instruction will require an investment of $10.9 billion in kindergarten through twelfth grade over the next four years. (See "Cost Work Sheet," pages 23–25.)

We estimate that $4.2 billion—or nearly 40 percent of the total—will be derived from existing appropriations, corporate and foundation grants, and volume-purchase discounts. Examples of such resources are the following:

- Funds currently provided through the California Education Technology Act
- State buys initiated by the California Technology Assistance Project
- The Computers for Schools Program, which coordinates the collection, repair, and distribution of donated computers
- One-time funds, such as the $279 million in the 1995 state Budget Act, distributed to all school districts on a per-pupil basis for nonrecurring expenditures, including the acquisition of technology

- Funds from Public Utilities Commission ratepayer settlements
- Grant programs sponsored by corporations and foundations
- Fund-raising efforts of local organizations

Solving the problem of raising funds of this magnitude is not solely a corporate responsibility. It is also a public responsibility. Although the efforts of business, organizations, and individuals will provide significant resources, the remaining $6.7 billion over a four-year period is a gap that must be filled from new public revenues.

Where will the additional money come from?

The [information] highway is going to give us all access to seemingly unlimited information, anytime and anyplace we care to use it. It's an exhilarating prospect, because putting this technology to use to improve education will lead to downstream benefits in every area of society.

Bill Gates, Chairman
and Chief Executive Officer
Microsoft Corporation

Funding

POTENTIAL SOURCES OF INCOME We recommend a funding portfolio that includes several potential sources, such as a broad sales tax; targeted taxes on videocassettes, software, and computers and peripherals; bonds initiated at the local, regional, and state levels; a surcharge on telecommunications users; taxes on utility users; an increased state income tax; and growth dividend funds that will automatically accrue to schools during an economic recovery.

We are heartened that the California Business Roundtable, an organization of 80 chief executive officers of California's major corporations, has agreed to convene a small group representing business, education, and public policy experts to explore the most expedient and pragmatic funding options for generating the $6.7 billion in new public funds needed to implement the report's recommendations. A task force subcommittee will continue participating in these education technology finance deliberations and will submit consensus recommendations to the Governor, the Legislature, and the State Superintendent of Public Instruction at the earliest possible date.

CUTTING THE PIE The total four-year technology budget will be apportioned as follows:

✓ Hardware and telecommunications infrastructure: $5.7 billion
✓ Learning resources and services: $2.9 billion
✓ Staff development and support: $2.3 billion (See Figure 3 and "Cost Work Sheet," pages 23–25.)

To ensure that funds will be available to meet the projected cost of an accelerated schedule for infrastructure development, equipment acquisition, and teacher training, funds should be targeted for technology and held separate from the aggregate education budget during the first four years.

Gradually increasing annual funding levels from 10 percent of the total in Year One to 40 percent of the total in Year Four will help encourage a more measured approach to disbursements. The lag time for phasing in full funding will give districts throughout the state time to put content and performance standards in place and to develop detailed plans for integrating technology at the local level. (See Figure 4.)

We expect to meet our objectives for bringing California schools into the top 10 percent of the states in technology by the year 2000. Once technology has become integral to the curricula it advances, ongoing technology expenditures—to replace and upgrade hardware and acquire new courseware that has since come onto the market—will no longer need to be a separate item in district budgets.

FIGURE 3

How Funds Will Be Spent in the First Four Years*

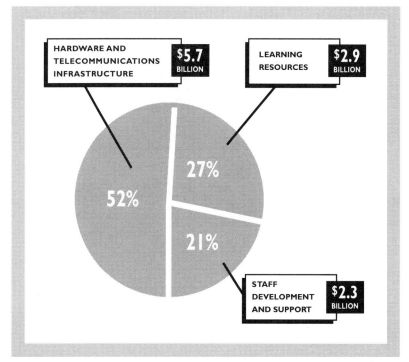

HARDWARE AND TELECOMMUNICATIONS INFRASTRUCTURE **$5.7 BILLION**

LEARNING RESOURCES **$2.9 BILLION**

52%

27%

21%

STAFF DEVELOPMENT AND SUPPORT **$2.3 BILLION**

*In subsequent years we anticipate that expenditures will be divided equally among the three categories.

Y ou cannot expect a faculty to rethink and change its schools without serious time and money, any more than General Motors thought it could build the Saturn without an upfront investment of more than eight years and billions of dollars.

Lewis Solmon, President
Milken Institute for Job & Capital Formation

A difficult problem remains: striking a balance between *have* and *have-not* schools. We know that a widening gap in student access to technology exists not only in schools, but also in homes and communities. How can we guarantee that all learning environments will meet statewide benchmarks for technology access without penalizing those communities that have led their peers in securing some measure of public or private support for putting children on a technology track? How can we make certain that homes and communities are equally linked to the technology we are proposing?

Analysts say that changes in the labor market, such as less demand for workers without technological skills, are contributing to

FIGURE 4

New Public Revenues Needed for Technology in K–12 Schools

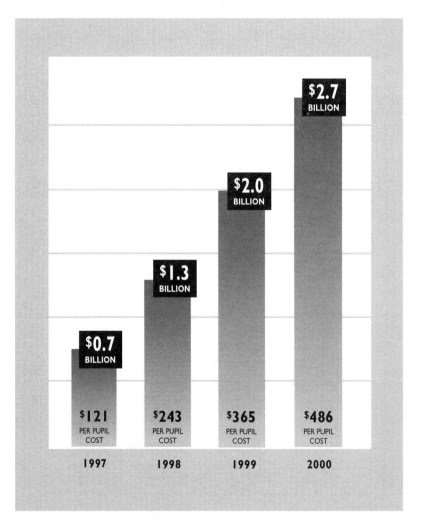

			$2.7 BILLION
		$2.0 BILLION	
	$1.3 BILLION		
$0.7 BILLION			
$121 PER PUPIL COST	$243 PER PUPIL COST	$365 PER PUPIL COST	$486 PER PUPIL COST
1997	1998	1999	2000

a growing income inequality between the rich and poor. Helping the poor get access to the technology they need to become successful is becoming increasingly difficult.

In an effort to devise an equitable strategy, we advise that funding be allocated according to a combination of formulas, including a per-pupil distribution, leadership grants, competitive merit grants, and aid for districts with special needs.

RETURN ON INVESTMENT

In the end a better question than "How much does it cost?" is "What benefits can we expect?" Although hard and fast numbers remain elusive, various studies demonstrate significant return on technology-related investments. For example, the Milken Institute for Job & Capital Formation estimates a return of $5 for every dollar invested in improving the technology know-how of California's labor force.

Another study by Alan Kruger, a Princeton economist, calculates that computer-savvy employees earned 10 percent to 15 percent more than their non-computer-literate colleagues; and recent data from the University of California at Davis Career Center lend support for the proposition that technological skills add hard economic value.

After reviewing the research, we have concluded that students familiar with computers and telecommunications from their early years will be more comfortable in later life using new technology for problem solving of all kinds. At the point at which our educational responsibilities end, we will have prepared our students more adequately than we do now to take their next steps into the future, wherever it leads—to a job or additional education.

Businesses are spending billions training people because they don't learn how to use technology in schools. From a national-policy perspective, there should be the highest priority around these issues.

Roy D. Pea, Dean
Northwestern University

Next Steps

REVEILLE We have, we hope, sounded a call to action for anyone concerned about the continued viability of public instruction: students, who need to discover both how to learn and what to learn; businesses, which require a constant stream of innovation; and community members, who consume the goods and services manufactured and provided by graduates of the state's schools.

Building the bridge between where we are and where we want to be four years from now will take a commitment from everyone involved with the educational system.

The demands of making California's public school children technology-ready recall massive government undertakings of earlier generations: the Rural Electrification Project of the 1930s, the GI Bill of the post-World War II era, and the Interstate Highway System of the 1950s. For all their organizational underpinnings, those programs were *sui generis*. Without precursors, they were spawned by need, founded on judgment, and steadied by commitment. The results propelled a nation forward.

Like those programs, California's proposed public school technology integration project is without precedent. No state or program has ever gone this way before. Uniqueness, however, does not diminish the necessity of staying the course. Measurable goals will be achieved not with piecemeal reform but with the coordinated advocacy of all concerned—students, parents, teachers, and administrators; government at all levels; businesses; and nonprofit organizations.

Recommended Actions

Although we know that many of you will be very creative in how you support technology integration, we ask that you give high priority to the immediate and future actions recommended in the matrix that follows.

	IMMEDIATE PRIORITY	FUTURE ACTION
Students	Demand appropriate technology in your classrooms. Actively support district and state technology initiatives.	Increase technology proficiency.
Teachers	Seek technology training opportunities, including those on the Internet, for meeting credentialing and the three-tier competencies. Advocate for more technology in the classroom by actively supporting district and state technology initiatives.	Incorporate technology into traditional curricula. Use electronic methods of sharing expertise with peers.
Parents/ Communities	Advocate for more technology in the classroom by actively supporting local and state technology initiatives.	Establish community-based technology application assistance centers to meet community needs.
Local School Boards	Develop a strategic plan for acquiring and integrating technology. Incorporate technology expertise into the teacher hiring and evaluation process. Adopt technology-based student content and performance standards for graduation.	Upgrade minimum hiring requirements. Institute appropriate incentives to encourage teachers to integrate technology into the curriculum.
School Administrators	Devise an action plan for acquiring benchmark technology. Develop new hiring criteria that incorporate technology expertise. Coordinate the adoption of the technology-based student content and performance standards.	Develop loaner programs to expand teacher, student, and family access to computers and E-mail. Expand personal use of computers and E-mail systems for planning and discharging administrative responsibilities. Involve the community in planning for technology.
County Offices of Education/ California Technology Assistance Project	Develop a master plan for coordinating and upgrading a statewide telecommunications infrastructure. Cooperate with the California Department of Education in creating databases for sharing information on students and school finance.	Coordinate submission of applications to federal funding sources. Develop a tool for schools to use in developing technology plans.
Employee Unions	Actively support district and state technology initiatives.	Support the development of teacher content and performance standards.

Recommended Actions (Continued)

	IMMEDIATE PRIORITY	FUTURE ACTION
Governor and Legislators	Provide schools full-scale funding for technology on a per-pupil basis, with adjustments for equity.	Fund research and development that provides guidance and assistance to public schools regarding technology acquisition and integration.
State Board of Education/ Education Council for Technology in Learning	Revise the instructional materials adoption process to foster technology integration. Recommend technology-based content and performance standards for teachers and students.	Support longitudinal studies of technology integration and student performance. Encourage the development of technology-based curriculum materials.
Commission on Teacher Credentialing/ Teacher Preparation Institutions	Require technology competency for granting and renewing teaching credentials. Require technology use in meeting course-work requirements.	Provide appropriate technology in college and university classrooms.
California Department of Education	Embed technology in curriculum frameworks. Develop technology-based content and performance standards for students and teachers. Spearhead statewide activities, such as NetDay. Incorporate technology into reading and mathematics initiatives, Challenge districts, the provisions of the Improving America's Schools Act, and special education programs.	Gather and report data benchmarking technology integration and its effects on scholastic progress. Provide a central information system on technology-related topics in collaboration with county offices of education. Coordinate purchasing activities to maximize economies of scale. Collaborate with the California Technology Assistance Project in preparing tools for schools to use in developing technology plans.
Businesses, Foundations, and Organizations (such as the Business Roundtable and the Industry Council for Technology in Learning)	Sponsor and support legislation to fund technology integration. Sponsor events and volunteer activities to promote technology awareness, including NetDay; Sign-on Day, where the school community signs onto the Internet; and Cyber-Camps, teacher and student technology camps.	Partner with local schools to find more cost-effective ways to provide technology. Develop measures to determine satisfaction with the technology expertise of high school graduates. Sponsor courseware development.
Public Utilities Commission	Represent school needs in Federal Communications Commission hearings regarding universal telecommunications services, Snow-Rockefeller provisions in the Telecommunications Act of 1996, the Small Business Development and Economic Development Fund, and others.	Develop affordable connect rates for schools.

Cost Work Sheet

FOUR-YEAR COSTS (1996 DOLLARS) TO REACH BENCHMARKS

Average school: 700 students
33 staff
29 rooms
(27 classrooms,
1 library-media
center, and 1 office)

Number of California schools: 7,818

	Benchmark Assumptions for Average School	Four-Year Cost for Average Room	Four-Year Cost for Average School	Four-Year Costs Statewide
I. Staff Development and Support				
A. Trainers	2,000 hours of training @ $35 per hour	$2,414	$70,000	$547,260,000
B. Staff support, materials, mileage, etc.	$2,000 per person (33 staff members)	$2,276	$66,000	$515,988,000
C. District/county technical support	.3 FTE = $15,000 per year for 4 years	$2,069	$60,000	$469,080,000
D. School site technical support	.5 FTE = $25,000 per year for 4 years	$3,448	$100,000	$781,800,000
Four-year total (staff development, etc.)		**$10,207**	**$296,000**	**$2,314,128,000**
Percent of total				**21%**
II. Learning Resources				
A. Computer software	$2,000 × 29 rooms for 4 years	$8,000	$232,000	$1,813,776,000
B. Upgrades	$200 × 29 rooms for 4 years	$800	$23,200	$181,377,600
C. Other multimedia materials and services	$500 × 29 rooms for 4 years	$2,000	$58,000	$453,444,000
D. Communications (connect charges, etc.)	$1,265 per month × 12 months for 4 years	$2,094	$60,720	$474,708,960
Four-year total (learning resources)		**$12,894**	**$373,920**	**$2,923,306,560**
Percent of total				**27%**

	Benchmark Assumptions for Average School	Four-Year Cost for Average Room	Four-Year Cost for Average School	Four-Year Costs Statewide
III. Hardware and Telecommunications Infrastructure				
A. Computers	6 computers @ $1,525 × 29 rooms	$9,150	$265,350	$2,074,506,300
B. Special interfaces	$700 for each of 29 rooms	$700	$20,300	$158,705,400
C. Scanners	$675 for each of 29 rooms	$675	$19,575	$153,037,350
D. Networked laser printers	$1,100 for each of 29 rooms	$1,100	$31,900	$249,394,200
E. Color printers	5 @ $400 (shared by 29 rooms)	$69	$2,000	$15,636,000
F. Audio recorders and players	5 @ $75 (shared by 29 rooms)	$13	$375	$2,931,750
G. Headphones	174 (one per computer) @ $30	$180	$5,220	$40,809,960
H. Liquid crystal presentation panels	5 @ $1,100 (shared by 29 rooms)	$190	$5,500	$42,999,000
I. Video capture boards	5 @ $350 (shared by 29 rooms)	$60	$1,750	$13,681,500
J. Video cameras	5 @ $600 (shared by 29 rooms)	$103	$3,000	$23,454,000
K. Videodisc players	5 @ $325 (shared by 29 rooms)	$56	$1,625	$12,704,250
L. Television monitors	$500 for each of 28 rooms	$483	$14,000	$109,452,000
M. Videocassette recorders and players	$350 for each of 28 rooms	$338	$9,800	$76,616,400
N. Overhead projectors and screens	$500 for each of 28 rooms	$483	$14,000	$109,452,000
O. Fax machines	2 @ $400 (shared by 29 rooms)	$27	$800	$6,254,400
P. Telephones	$50 for each of 28 rooms	$48	$1,400	$10,945,200
Q. High-speed copiers	2 @ $5,000	$345	$10,000	$78,180,000
R. Telecommunications infrastructure	$74,000 per school	$2,552	$74,000	$578,532,000
S. Furniture and security equipment	$2,700 for each of 29 rooms	$2,700	$78,300	$612,149,400
Four-year total (hardware, etc.)		**$19,272**	**$558,895**	**$4,369,441,110**
Percent of total				**40%**
IV. Maintenance, Upgrades, and Replacements (15% of Installed Hardware)		**$5,844**	**$169,475**	**$1,324,955,732**
Percent of total				**12%**
Grand total (four years)		**$48,217**	**$1,398,290**	**$10,931,831,402**

FOUR-YEAR COSTS AND FUNDING SOURCES

Existing appropriations	$1,623,376,963
Corporate and foundation grants	$874,546,512
Volume purchase discounts	$1,749,093,025
New public funds required	$6,684,814,902
Total costs to reach benchmarks	**$10,931,831,402**

ANNUAL NEW PUBLIC FUNDS REQUIRED FOR FOUR-YEAR PHASE-IN

Year	New public funds	Per-student cost
Year 1 (10%)	$668,481,490	$121
Year 2 (20%)	$1,336,962,980	$243
Year 3 (30%)	$2,005,444,471	$365
Year 4 (40%)	$2,673,925,961	$486
Totals	**$6,684,814,902**	**$1,215**

Bibliography

Advanced Telecommunications in U.S. Public Schools, K–12. Prepared by the Office of Educational Research and Improvement, U.S. Department of Education. NCES 95-731. Washington, D.C.: U.S. Government Printing Office, 1995. Available via www: [http://www.ed.gov/NCES/index.html]

America's Children and the Information Superhighway: A Briefing Book and National Action Agenda. Santa Monica, Calif.: The Children's Partnership, 1994.

Apple Computer, Inc. *Changing the Conversation About Teaching, Learning, and Technology: A Report on 10 Years of ACOT Research.* Cupertino, Calif.: Apple Computer, Inc., 1995. Available via www: [http://www.atg.apple.com/acot/index.html]

Building the Future: K–12 Network Technology Planning Guide. Sacramento: California Department of Education, 1994. Available via www: [http://goldmine. cde.ca.gov/www/Technology/k–12/NTPG/NTPG.html]

The California Master Plan for Educational Technology. Prepared by the California Planning Commission for Educational Technology. Sacramento: California Department of Education, 1992.

Children and the Information Superhighway: Corporate Leadership and Action. Santa Monica, Calif.: The Children's Partnership, 1995.

Clinton, Bill. "Remarks by the President to the Concord [California] Community on Netday." White House Press Release, March 9, 1996. Available via www: [http: www.whitehouse.gov]

Dwyer, David. "Apple Classrooms of Tomorrow: What We've Learned," *Educational Leadership* (April, 1994), 4–10.

Gates, Bill. *The Road Ahead.* New York: Viking Penguin, 1995.

Getting Results. Sacramento: The Governor's Council on Information Technology, 1995. Available via www: [http://www.ca.gov]

Glennan, Thomas K., and Arthur Melmed. *Fostering the Use of Educational Technology: Elements of a National Strategy.* Santa Monica, Calif.: RAND, 1996. Available via www: [http://www.rand.org]

Honey, Margaret, and Andres Henriquez. *Telecommunications and K–12 Educators: Findings from a National Study.* New York: Center for Technology in Education, Bank Street College of Education, 1993.

KickStart Initiative: Connecting America's Communities to the Information Superhighway. Prepared by the United States Advisory Council on the National Information Infrastructure. Washington, D.C.: U.S. Government Printing Office, 1996. Available via www: [http://www.benton.org/kickstart/]

Learning a Living: A Blueprint for High Performance. A SCANS Report for America 2000. Washington, D.C.: The Secretary's Commission on Achieving Necessary Skills, U.S. Department of Labor, 1992.

Logan, Kaki, and Pat Gemma. "Technology in Secondary School Reform," *California Technology Project Quarterly,* Vol. 2, No. 2 (Winter, 1991), 24–27.

Lucas, George. "Letter from the Chairman," *Edutopia* (Summer, 1996).

Making It Happen: Report of the Secretary's Conference on Educational Technology. Washington, D.C.: Office of Educational Technology, U.S. Department of Education, 1995.

Mehlinger, Howard. "Achieving School Reform Through Technology," *TECHNOS: Quarterly for Education and Technology,* Vol. 5, No. 1 (Spring, 1996), 26–29.

Mergendoller, John R., and others. *Exemplary Approaches to Training Teachers to Use Technology.* Vol. 1. NTIS No. 95-170932. Springfield, Va.: National Technical Information Service, 1994.

Reich, Robert. "The Fracturing of the Middle Class," *New York Times,* August 31, 1994.

Riley, Richard. "Press Briefing by Secretary of Education Richard Riley." Blue Ribbon Schools Awards Ceremony, May 29, 1996.

Rising to the Challenge: A New Agenda for California Schools and Communities. Denver, Colo.: Education Commission of the States, 1995.

Sivin-Kachala, Jay, and Ellen R. Bialo. *Report on the Effectiveness of Technology in Schools, '95-'96.* Washington, D.C.: Software Publishers Association, 1995. Available via www: [http://www.spa.org/project/edu_pub/pbtop/htm]

Solmon, Lewis. "The Last Silver Bullet: Technology Can Save Our Schools." Santa Monica, Calif.: Milken Institute for Job and Capital Formation, 1995 (unpublished manuscript).

Technical Guidebook for Schools. Santa Clara, Calif.: Smart Valley, Inc., 1995. Available via www: [http://www.svi.org/netday/welcome/]

Technology in Public Schools, 14th Edition: Installed Base Technology in U.S. Public Schools, Covering 1981–1995. Denver, Colo.: Quality Education Data, Inc., 1995.

Technology's Role in Education Reform. Prepared by Barbara Means and Kerry Olson for the Office of Educational Research and Improvement, U.S. Department of Education. Menlo Park, Calif.: SRI International, 1995.

Telecommunications Infrastructure for K–12 Schools and Public Libraries. Prepared by California Senate Bill 600 Task Force. San Francisco: Public Utilities Commission, 1995.

Telecommunications Technology and Education: What Have We Learned from Research and Experience? Prepared by John Cradler and Elizabeth Bridgforth, Far West Laboratory, for the California Department of Education and the Telemation Project. San Francisco: Far West Laboratory for Educational Research and Development, [1995].

United States Education and Instruction Through Telecommunications: Distance Learning for All Learners. Washington, D.C.: Council of Chief State School Officers, 1995.

U.S. Congress, Office of Technology Assessment. *Teachers and Technology: Making the Connection.* OTA-EHR-616. Washington, D.C.: U.S. Government Printing Office, 1995.

What Work Requires of Schools. A SCANS Report for America 2000. Washington, D.C.: The Secretary's Commission on Achieving Necessary Skills, U.S. Department of Labor, 1991.

Williams, Paul L., and others. *1994 NAEP Reading: A First Look.* Prepared by Educational Testing Service under contract with the National Center for Education Statistics. Washington, D.C.: U.S. Department of Education, Office of Educational Research and Improvement, 1995.

Wujcik, Anne, and Nelson B. Heller. *Schools and Education: On-Ramps to Opportunities on the Information Superhighway.* Highland Park, Ill.: Nelson B. Heller & Associates, 1995.

Publications Available from the Department of Education

This publication is one of over 600 that are available from the California Department of Education. Some of the more recent publications or those most widely used are the following:

Item no.	Title (Date of publication)	Price
1204	Adult Education Handbook for California (1995 Edition)	$11.50
1163	The Arts: Partnerships as a Catalyst for Educational Reform (1994)	10/10.00*
1166	Building the Future: K–12 Network Technology Planning Guide (1994)	11.75
1219	California Private School Directory, 1995-96 (1996)	17.50
1220	California Public School Directory (1996)	17.50
1273	California Special Education Programs: A Composite of Laws (1996)	no charge
0488	Caught in the Middle: Educational Reform for Young Adolescents in California Public Schools (1987)	7.50
1264	Challenging Standards for Student Success (1995)	13.52
1179	Continuation Education in California Public Schools (1995)	7.25
1093	Differentiating the Core Curriculum and Instruction to Provide Advanced Learning Opportunities (1994)	6.50
1215	English-as-a-Second-Language Handbook for Adult Education Instructors, 1995 Edition (1995)	9.75
0041	English–Language Arts Framework for California Public Schools (1987)	5.50
0927	English–Language Arts Model Curriculum Standards: Grades Nine Through Twelve (1991)	6.50
1244	Every Child a Reader: The Report of the California Reading Task Force (1995)	4.50†
0804	Foreign Language Framework for California Public Schools (1989)	6.50
1083	Handbook for Teaching Vietnamese-Speaking Students (1994)	5.50‡
1253	Health Adoption Report: Review of Instructional Resources Submitted to the State Board of Education, Kindergarten Through Grade Eight (1995)	7.25
1064	Health Framework for California Public Schools, Kindergarten Through Grade Twelve (1994)	8.50
0737	Here They Come: Ready or Not—Report of the School Readiness Task Force (summary report) (1988)	4.50
0712	History–Social Science Framework for California Public Schools (1988)	7.75
1154	Home Economics Education Career Path Guide and Model Curriculum Standards (1994)	17.00
1140	I Can Learn: A Handbook for Parents, Teachers, and Students (1994)	8.00
1245	Improving Mathematics Achievement for All California Students: The Report of the California Mathematics Task Force (1995)	4.50†
1178	Independent Study Operations Manual, 1993 Revised Edition with 1994 Updates (1994)	30.00
1258	Industrial and Technology Education: Career Path Guide and Model Curriculum Standards (1996)	16.00

* Ten copies is the minimum number that can be ordered. For more than 10 copies, the price is 70 cents each for up to 99 copies, 50 cents each for 100 or more copies.

† For orders of ten or more copies, the price is $4.00 each for 10 to 99 copies, $2.50 each for 100 or more copies.

‡ Also available at the same price for students who speak Cantonese, Japanese, Korean, Pilipino, and Portuguese.

Prices are subject to change. Please call 1-800-995-4099 for current prices and shipping charges.

Item no.	Title (Date of publication)	Price
1269	Instructional Materials Approved for Legal Compliance, 1996 Edition	$22.00
1147	It's Elementary! (Abridged Version) (1994)	3.50*
1024	It's Elementary! Elementary Grades Task Force Report (1992)	7.00
1266	Literature for the Visual and Performing Arts, Kindergarten Through Grade Twelve (1996)	9.50
1216	Martin Luther King, Jr., 1929–1968 (1995)	7.00
1033	Mathematics Framework for California Public Schools, 1992 Edition	7.50
1183	Meeting the Challenge: A History of Adult Education in California—From the Beginnings to the 1990s (1995)	12.50
1144	Moral, Civic, and Ethical Education Handbook (1995)	9.50
1065	Physical Education Framework for California Public Schools, Kindergarten Through Grade Twelve (1994)	6.75
1221	Practical Ideas for Teaching Writing as a Process at the Elementary School and Middle School Levels (1996 Revised Edition)	17.00
1094	Program Quality Review Training Materials for Elementary and Middle Level Schools (1994)	7.50
1118	Roads to the Future: Final Report (1994)	10.00
1117	Roads to the Future: Summary Report (1994)	8.00
1191	Safe Schools: A Planning Guide for Action (1995 Edition)	10.75
1246	School Attendance Review Boards Handbook: Operations and Resources (1995)	6.50
0870	Science Framework for California Public Schools (1990)	8.00
1040	Second to None: A Vision of the New California High School (1992)	6.50
1276	Teaching Reading: A Balanced, Comprehensive Approach to Teaching Reading in Prekindergarten Through Grade Three (1996)	5.25
1260	Today's Special: A Fresh Approach to Meals for Preschoolers (video and guide) (1996)	16.00†
1261	Visual and Performing Arts Framework for California Public Schools, Kindergarten Through Grade Twelve (1996)	14.00

* Single price applies to quantities up to eight copies. For more than eight copies, the price is $3.00 each for up to 99 copies, $2.00 each for 100–249 copies, $1.50 each for 250–499 copies, $1.00 each for 500 or more copies.

† Also available in a Spanish edition of both video and guide (item no. 1262) at same price.

Orders should be directed to:

California Department of Education
Bureau of Publications, Sales Unit
P.O. Box 271
Sacramento, CA 95812-0271

Please include the item number and desired quantity for each title ordered. Shipping and handling charges are additional, and purchasers in California also add sales tax.

Mail orders must be accompanied by a check, a purchase order, or a credit card number, including expiration date (VISA or MasterCard only). Purchase orders without checks are accepted from educational institutions, businesses, and governmental agencies. Telephone orders will be accepted toll-free (1-800-995-4099) for credit card purchases. *All sales are final.*

The *Educational Resources Catalog* contains illustrated, annotated listings of departmental publications, videos, and other instructional materials. Free copies of the *Catalog* may be obtained by writing to the address given above or by calling (916) 445-1260.

Prices are subject to change. Please call 1-800-995-4099 for current prices and shipping charges.

95-53 CR 651155 7-96 23M